Rocky

The Awesome Dog!

Capt. Ed Sullivan

authorHOUSE®

AuthorHouse™
1663 Liberty Drive
Bloomington, IN 47403
www.authorhouse.com
Phone: 1 (800) 839-8640

Published by AuthorHouse 08/24/2018

ISBN: 978-1-5462-5577-2 (sc)
ISBN: 978-1-5462-5576-5 (e)

Print information available on the last page.

This book is printed on acid-free paper.

Table of Contents

About the book...

"ROCKY THE AWESOME Dog," is a story about the love and companionship shared between a young boy named Ryan Sullivan and his faithful dog named "Rocky." The childhood years of youth seem to pass by quickly from our memory.

This story is a reflection on those precious years of youth that Ryan & Rocky shared growing up in the forest of South Plymouth, Massachusetts. Recalling a boy and his dog blossoming like a flower amidst the ancient Indian hunting grounds of the Great Herring Pond Indian tribe.

Rocky was from a champion German Shephard kennel across the street from New England Patriots Stadium in Foxboro, but due to his light tan coat of fur Rocky was not wanted as a show dog. So on Christmas Day Rocky was united with Ryan by Santa Claus igniting the youthful exuberance of a young boy and an adorable puppy.

Due to an unforeseen circumstance in their teenager years Rocky had to leave Ryan and his home in the forest. It was a sad day that ended the innocence of youth between a boy and his dog.

However many years later a letter to Ryan's dad arrived from a new owner of Rocky. And the Sullivan family would learn and be able to share with any children that would read this book the story of the incredible life of "Rocky the Awesome Dog!"

ONCE UPON A time there was a little boy named Ryan and his dog named Rocky.

Ryan & Rocky lived in the woods on dusty Roxy Cahoon Road.

Ryan & Rocky loved to run through the forest and fish in their Great Herring pond the biggest of Plymouth's 365 ponds!

Rocky the awesome dog was Ryan's loyal companion growing up together in their Cedarville forest home!

ON A WINTRY Christmas morning Santa Claus brought "Rocky the Awesome Puppy Dog" to Ryan's forest home.

Santa Claus appeared on Christmas morning at Ryan's snow laden Roxy Cahoon Road home in Plymouth, Massachusetts wintry forest. In the porch window the little boy Ryan glowed with great joy seeing Santa on his porch with a puppy dog. "Boy Oh Boy, Ryan got a big surprise….a new puppy all ready to play…..wagging his tail in Ryan's door on Christmas morn'!

Ryan shouted, "Santa is awesome!" He brought me what I always wanted my own puppy dog!" Funny Ryan burst with laughter for all, saying "Daddy Santa looks like old Mr. Donahue my school bus driver!"

As Santa Claus whisked off the front porch to return to his sleigh, he winked, and waved a special goodbye to Ryan that day!

In a very loud cheer Santa shouted, "Ho Ho Ho!" May a Merry Christmas be had by one and all!" Turning with a big beautiful smile, Ryan hugged his new puppy and kissed his fur, then shouted, "That's right Santa, Ho Ho Ho, and Merry Christmas be had by one and all."

RYAN & ROCKY lived on Roxy Cahoon Road, a sandy road behind Great Herring Pond.

Ryan loved his dog Rocky! Ryan took Rocky out to play every day.

Ryan brushed Rocky's fur real nice, and always gave Rocky lots of hugs!

Ryan fed Rocky his dog food every night and always got a thank you from Rocky's long pink tongue lapping "thank you" on Ryan's smiling face. Ryan always remembered to give Rocky a bowl of fresh cool water after they ran together in the woods.

As little boys Ryan & Rocky grew up having fun in a forest wonderland known as Cedarville!

ONE DAY AUNTIE Jade, Ryan's little brown mouse sister, came crying in the kitchen saying "Daddy, if Ryan can have that awesome pup Rocky? Why can't I have this cuddly Oreo cookie cat? So Jade the biggest sister down on Roxy Cahoon Road, got her big wish, an Oreo cookie cat! It was amazing that Jade's cat "cookie" got along just so well with Rocky.

Rocky & Cookie never fought like regular cat and dogs. Ryan & Jade taught them love!

Jade loved her cat "Cookie," and sometimes played dolls with "Cookie" in her pink walled room!

Sometimes early in the morning if you quietly tip-toed downstairs you could be one of the lucky kids to see "Cookie" sleeping between Rocky's front paws on cold winter mornings!

ONE DAY INTO the oak wooded study came the "littlest Auntie Kate" along with her hero, and protector, her big brother Ryan!

Kate said, if Jade can have that "cookie" cat, and Ryan can have that awesome dog "Rocky" "Why can't I have one of the wild kitty cats that live under our St. Bonaventure's Church?

So after church the "Littlest Kate," and her big brother Ryan, with Father Kelly went scurrying around under the church and caught a little wild (feral) kitten for Kate.

Kate's kitty was very shy and slept in the leaves under our porch. Kate's kitty always followed Jade's cat "Cookie" wherever Cookie went. "Cookie" was like Kate's kitty's big sister!

ON A WARM summer day another of Ryan's sisters Auntie Brooks came walking off the front porch and said, "Hey Daddy, if Ryan can have that awesome Dog "Rocky", and Jade can have that Oreo "Cookie" cat? And Kate can have her "Wild" kitty cat?"

Why can't I have this little Maggie terrier? So on that day little Brooks who always played like Davy Crockett around her forest home, finally got her wish, a little "Maggie" puppy dog!

Brooks was known as "Brooksie Doo" and she taught her pup "Maggie" to protect her home like a little general in the

Army! "Maggie" slept on "Rocky's" porch and always chased the coyotes into the woods when they tried to sneak up and steal food from the dog's bowl.

Auntie Brooks and her dog Maggie grew up in the Cedarville woods together, and then traveled as young adventurous teenagers together across the United States to the Pacific Ocean!

Ever since Uncle Jack was a little boy he always dreamed of getting a young puppy dog like Ryan's pup "Rocky" who came to our house on Christmas day!

Dreams of a young cuddly cute puppy dog danced in little Jack's head as he watched Rocky & Ryan play on that wintry Christmas morning when Santa Claus brought Rocky to our home!

THEN ONE BEAUTIFUL summer day Uncle Jack, said, "Hey Daddy, if Ryan can have that awesome dog "Rocky," why can't I have my own little pup named Bear?

So on that summer day, Ryan's little brother known as "Jacker" got his own puppy which he called "Bear" because he was so cuddly like Jack's teddy bear. "Jacker" got his wish, his "Bear!"

Uncle Jack's "Bear" was the son of Ryan's dog "Rocky." "Bear" grew up at the Roxy Cahoon home with his daddy "Rocky" and his mom "Shadow." Jack and his pup "Bear" ran through the forest and played every day behind Jack's big brother Ryan and "Bear's" daddy "Rocky!"

THE TOWN ARTIST always saw Jack hugging his puppy dog "Bear," and honored their loyalty for each other by painting a picture of them hugging in a field one day.

E<small>VERY SUMMER AS</small> "Rocky" and Ryan grew they always let little brother Jack play with them!

BIG BROTHER RYAN would always look out for his little sisters and would teach Rocky how to protect his sisters with Karate at their Roxy Cahoon home!

ALL THE KIDS loved to go fishing with Ryan & Rocky! Across the dirt road and down the path in the woods was Plymouth's Great Herring Pond where Ryan taught his brother and sisters how to catch fish!

ONE DAY IT was said all through Plymouth schools that the Sullivan's dogs Rocky & Shadow had a big litter of puppies. The five Sullivan kids played with their favorite puppy dogs every day! One of those pups would be Uncle Jack's Bear!

MANY DAYS "ROCKY" and Ryan would run through the path in the Cedarville forest that led to Great Grandma Mary and Great Grandpa Jack Lynn's home! Ryan would always get a cookie treat from his Grandma Mary, and Grandpa Jack would give Rocky a cool bowl of water.

On many other days "Rocky and Ryan would run through another path in the Cedarville forest that led to Great Grandma Anne and Great Grandpa Ed Sullivan's home! Ryan would always get a cold hoodsie ice cream from Grandma Anne, and Rocky would always get a dog bone from Grandpa Ed Sullivan Sr.

For many of Ryan & Rocky's birthdays Grandma & Grandpa Lynn, and Grandma & Grandpa Sullivan would come from their homes next door to celebrate Ryan and all the kids birthdays in the big kitchen off the porch.

ONE DAY A Sullivan and Ryan family reunion was planned on the nine acre Roxy Cahoon home. Since Timothy Sullivan arrived in Boston from Ireland in 1850 nobody had a Sullivan / Ryan family reunion party till now!

Ryan Sullivan a young teenager had both family member's names. Ryan was named after his great grandmother Mary Ellen "Nellie" Ryan. Over 400 Sullivan's from all across America. And all of the Ryan's descendants of the 7 Ryan Sisters came from Newfoundland.

And as the O'Reilly's Irish band began the Sullivan/Ryan Reunion with a slow Irish waltz out from the crowd to begin the 1st dance stepped 90 year old Aunt Clara Ryan from

New York, and Ryan Sullivan from Plymouth dancing as all his teary eyed cousins watched the kick-off to a week-long celebration of the Sullivan's and the Ryan's. Aunt Clara Ryan was the little sister to Ryan Sullivan's great grandmother Nellie Ryan!

The Sullivan's and the Ryan's were invited for 3 days to celebrate the genealogy done by cousin's Patty & Eddy Sullivan outlining the history of the Sullivan's since landing in America 168 years ago from Ireland.

The Sullivan's and the Ryan's celebrated for more than the 3 days on the invitation. For 7 days the cousin's camped throughout the Cedarville forest, and along the Cape Cod Canal making the Sullivan/Ryan reunion a memorable time had by all.

Irish family gathers in Cedarville

By Maggie Mills
Old Colony Memorial staff

PLYMOUTH — Four hundred members of the Sullivan-Ryan clan came together recently for their first family reunion in the woods off Roxy Cahoon Road in Cedarville.

Ed Sullivan said he and his wife, Heather, and cousin, Patricia Sullivan of Wollaston, worked months to co-ordinate the event, searching for family members to invite to the reunion, which was held on his nine-acre wooded lot in the middle of what he described as "God's country."

"We sent monthly letters and they came by plane, bus, private cars and motor trailers from all over the country, Canada and the Orient, with Pat booking rooms for the weekend at hotels, motels and camping grounds," said Sullivan, who explained he is the seventh son of a seventh son. His mother, Nellie Ryan Sullivan, called South Boston her home.

Sullivan, 34, is a disabled merchant marine sailor who went to sea at the age of 17. He said the three-day reunion in the weekend of Aug. 12 took place beneath two tents set up alongside the long porch which circles his four-year-old ranch house.

Throughout the weekend the clan mixed, ate, drank, reminisced, and exchanged family data.

When the matriarch of the family, Clara Ryan, 88, of Brooklyn, N.Y., stepped down from her Winnebago to dance with Sullivan's 10-year-old son, Ryan, to Irish music played by the O'Reillys, her family from Newfoundland whooped and whistled while clapping in time.

Among the special guests, was Frank Sullivan, an Army ranger from Weymouth who flew in full uniform from Korea just to be present, Sullivan said.

Sullivan said Sunday was a special day for the family, most of them Catholics. The Rev. Robert Buchan, S.J., a teacher at Boston College, and a helper at St. Bonaventure Church in Manomet for 31 years, was the family's guest that day.

REUNION — Ed and Heather Sullivan with their five children welcomed 400 family members at a reunion at their home on Roxy Cahoon Road in Cedarville. Sullivan holds Jack Patrick. The other children, from left, are Brooks, Ryan, Kate and Jade. (Staff photo by Maggie Mills.)

Sullivan said he had to leave his work on the sea. With time on his hand, he made the decision to research the Sullivan-Ryan family's genealogy after he attended a funeral of his uncle Paul Sullivan in Charlestown last winter. "During a conversation with some cousins, we said we only get together at funerals, why not some affair where we can have a good time," he said. "That started us reseaching the family background."

Sullivan said that between therapy treatments for his injured legs and back, he worked on the family

Sullivan, came on the S.S. Plymouth Rock from Ireland to this country in 1853.

"Timothy had a son, Patrick, who had a son, Jack. Jack had a son, Ed, who had Ed Jr., that's me, and I have a son we called Ryan Sullivan," Sullivan said. "Ryan is named for both sides, the Ryans and the Sullivans. He's our oldest of our five kids. Jade is 7. She was named for a stone I picked up in China, Kate is 6; Brooks, 4, has my mother's maiden name, and Jack Patrick is almost 2.

"I'm sure glad of my heritage. It's what President Kennedy once said,

whence we came," said Sullivan.

"Remember to write it took 130 years for the Sullivans to get out of the mudflats and rooming houses in (Southie) to Cedarville. And I built my house with my own two hands. Write that," he said.

JACK'S BIG BROTHER Ryan was nice and always took his puppy "Bear" out to play and poo with "Rocky" on snowy days!

On one of those snowy days many of the Sullivan kids like elves in the upstairs windows say they saw Ryan, Rocky, & puppy Bear playing with Santa Claus one bright wintry day!

ONE DAY A man from our church in nearby Manomet asked if Rocky wanted to meet a girlfriend "Fluffy" his pure white German Shepherd?

"Rocky" visited "Fluffy" in Manomet. They ran along Plymouth's White Horse Beach together. Rocky and Fluffy played and played and then one day we learned Fluffy was going to have puppies, and Rocky was the Daddy!

THROUGHOUT ALL THE years everyone always remembers the fond memories of Rocky and Ryan growing up as they played every day at their Roxy Cahoon home in the forest!

ONE DAY OUT of the blue a wandering girl came into the yard and tried to pick up Rocky by his hind legs while he was sleeping! This surprise on Rocky sleeping became a very sad day!

As THE WANDERING girl tried to pick up Rocky he jumped up startled from sleep and growled. The girl fell upside down and landed on a couple of Rocky's sharp teeth sticking out from his open mouth.

Rocky's tooth holes on the girl brought lawyers and insurance people to the Roxy Cahoon Road home. Legal things happened. Because of these legal things Rocky and Shadow the mother of Rocky's puppies must move away or else the house would have to be sold.

Grandpa Sullivan sent "Rocky" to dog heaven in Blackstone, Massachusetts!

It was one of the saddest days in the life of young Ryan Sullivan. Rocky & Ryan grew up together running through the forest and swimming in the pond nearby. Ryan cried and cried and hugged his dog Rocky, while Jade, Kate, Brooks, and Jack gave goodbye hugs to Shadow the momma dog.

After many weeks Grandpa Ed Sullivan Jr., found a happy ending for "Rocky" and a solution for the sadness of the Sullivan children.

Grandpa Ed Sullivan was going to send "Rocky" to dog heaven in Blackstone, Massachusetts!

THE FARM OF Mrs. Ginny McCoy in Blackstone, Massachusetts was dog heaven for "Rocky!" Ginny had a German shepherd breeding farm in the barn behind her home. Farmer Ginny McCoy needed a Daddy dog for all the girl shepherd dogs!

On the sad day Rocky went to his new home the telephone rang at two o'clock in the morning at the Sullivan home. Ginny McCoy told Grandpa Sullivan that Rocky arriving at his new home immediately jumped the fence into the barn.

Rocky was the happiest dog in the world, doing his job of kissing & hugging all the girl German shepherd dogs in her barn. Farmer Ginny McCoy said, "Truly Rocky went to Dog Heaven!"

Many years went by at the Sullivan's Roxy Cahoon Road home. The Sullivan kids always remembered Ryan's awesome dog named "Rocky."

Auntie Jade's cat "Cookie" became the oldest pet in the Roxy Cahoon home.

Uncle Jack's pup "Bear" grew up to look just like Rocky. Sometimes Ryan would sit on the porch petting "Bear" and be sad thinking about Bear's dad Rocky.

Bear ran around the house just like "Rocky" use to do chasing rabbits and deer that tried to eat his green grass lawn.

Nobody knows what happened to Auntie Kate's wild cat that lived in the leaves under the porch. The wild cat was so shy she just wandered off in the woods one day without saying goodbye!

But, Auntie Brooks dog "Maggie" became a new found terrorist in the home. She ran along the back of the couch barking out the window at anyone that was outside. Maggie would sleep on Brooks's big brother Ryan's chest on the couch. Brooks said it was OK so Ryan could get love from Maggie after missing his "Rocky" dog so much!

Maggie was very alert and chased anyone or any critter that came into our yard from the woods. One day Maggie chased a coyote dog that tried to sneak food from her dog bowl near the porch. It was a trick by the coyotes. The one coyote dog got Maggie to chase her deep in the woods where a whole pack of coyote dogs attacked Maggie and bit her bum up real bad. Brooks was crying real bad as she and her Daddy leaned over bloody Maggie at the doggie doctor's hospital. It would cost weeks of Daddy Sullivan's pay to have Maggie's ripped fur stitched up from the bloody mess made by the coyote's teeth.

Auntie Brooks was so happy to be able to have more fun days with Maggie at her Roxy Cahoon home. One day after Brooks got big she planned a journey across the country to California with her beloved dog "Maggie!"

Maggie was the most loyal dog to Brooks. Brooks became the only one that could hug Maggie because she became a nervous nipper always dreaming that people were coyotes trying to get her during sleep time.

Brooks and Maggie grew up as kids swimming in the Atlantic Ocean on Cape Cod Bay.

As young teenage girls Brooks and Maggie made it across America and swam in the faraway Pacific Ocean together!

Brooks taught Maggie to surf on her board at the beach, and promised Maggie no coyote's would get her in sunny California!

Many years passed by at the Sullivan home. At least a dozen years since Ryan's dog "Rocky" had gone away to dog heaven at the Blackstone farm of Ginny McCoy.

One day a letter came to Grandpa Ed Sullivan in the mail box. The letter was from a man named Mr. Wilson. Charley Wilson was the next door neighbor of Rocky's new owner Ginny McCoy in Blackstone, Massachusetts.

Mr. Wilson said, although we never met he heard so many wonderful things about the Sullivan family from his neighbor Ginny McCoy.

Ginny told Mr. Wilson the Sullivan's dog "Rocky" was the best dog she ever had. "Rocky" became the Daddy dog to her German shepherd breeding business. Rocky was the Daddy to hundreds of puppies born to the girl shepherds in dog kennel next to Mr. Wilson's home.

Mr. Wilson asked Ginny McCoy one day that if she ever went out of the dog business he would love to get that awesome dog Rocky, if he ever needed a new home.

Mr. Wilson wrote in his letter that one day Ginny McCoy broke her hip and could no longer run her dog business. She called Mr. Wilson over and asked if he would make a good home for "Rocky" her favorite dog?

In his long letter Mr. Wilson let me know about the wonderful life he and his 12 children had with Rocky the awesome dog!

Rocky was a good natured dog with Charley Wilson's kids. Rocky played in their yard with the children and walked them to the school bus at the end of the driveway every day.

Mr. Wilson wrote that one day he needed heart surgery and a long stay in the hospital till he got well. Rocky missed Mr. Wilson at home and was a good guard dog watching over his children while he rested at the hospital. The doctor told Mr. Wilson it would be good therapy for his heart to walk the country roads of the Blackstone every day with his loyal dog Rocky.

Mr. Wilson and Rocky walked the country roads getting healthier and stronger every day. Rocky loved the fresh air and spending this quiet morning time with Mr. Wilson sniffing every leaf and tree.

ONE DAY MR. Wilson as he walked the country road in Blackstone saw a baby cub bear sitting at the edge of the road in the grass. Mr. Wilson and Rocky walked carefully up to the baby cub bear sensing it was lost from its Mommy.

SUDDENLY JUST AS Mr. Wilson was going to pick up
the baby bear and bring it home, a big roar came from the
nest of trees nearby.

The big Mama Bear with big teeth and big black bear
claws came charging down on top of Mr. Wilson from the
wooded forest.

Suddenly bursting into the air "Rocky" jumped in front
of Mr. Wilson and continued to soar through the air until
he bit the big Mama Bear in the chest. The Mama Bear was
stopped from her ferocious attack on Mr. Wilson from the
big brave Rocky dog!

ROCKY WAS GROWLING really loud kept barking in front of Mr. Wilson and chased the Mama Bear and the baby bear cub back into the forest.

Mr. Wilson, who just had open heart surgery stood stunned looking at "Rocky" who had just saved his life. Mr. Wilson getting his breath bent over and patted Rocky on the head. Mr. Wilson in the silence of the wooded forest said, "Rocky I am truly thankful to have you! Your such an "Awesome Dog."

WHEN THE MAMA Bear got a safe distance away in the woods with her baby bear she turned and looked back one more time at the brave Rocky dog who protected Mr. Wilson. The Mama Bear then disappeared into the Blackstone forest with her baby bear.

THE TOWN ARTIST painted the famous story of "Rocky the Awesome Dog" saving Mr. Charley Wilson's life from that big black Bear one day in the Blackstone, Massachusetts forest!

INSIDE MR. WILSON'S letter to Grandpa Ed Sullivan was a picture of "Rocky" and the Wilson children hugging Rocky in front of the fireplace at the Wilson's Christmas decorated Blackstone home.

The Christmas picture was a great surprise as ever since Rocky came to the Sullivan home we made Christmas pictures with him in front of the fireplace and tree.

It was such a delightful story to hear of Rocky's amazing life after so many years.

It was a true gift to see the picture of the very happy Wilson kids hugging Rocky on Christmas Day, thankful that Rocky saved their Daddy from that big black Bear.

It brought tears to all the Sullivan family eyes recalling Santa Claus bringing Rocky to Ryan many Christmas's ago!

Staring at such a happy ending to Mr. Wilson's letter made Grandpa Sullivan say truly

"Rocky" was an Awesome Dog!"

AFTERWARD
Rocky the Awesome Dog!

The book "Rocky the Awesome Dog" is dedicated to my son Ryan Sullivan and my grandchildren Declan, Jack, and their sister little Ryan.

Rocky the Awesome Dog was originally written for Declan and Jack but changed after an unexpected call last November. For Declan, Jack, and their sister little Ryan this story is an effort to share a glimpse into some of the happy days of your Dad's youth spent with his childhood dog Rocky.

Going down memory lane with Ryan's pictures was a venue for me to begin the process to heal over the unexpected loss of such a young, strong, healthy son.

May Ryan's children come to learn that storytelling from our Sullivan native Ireland was intended for those who were too young to remember, and for the kids that were not yet born.

In Ireland it is called a gift of the gab, and Timothy Sullivan brought it to Boston from Ireland. And Ryan Sullivan brought it to Oregon from Boston. The Irish passed down stories just like the native Indians in the Old West.

The thought of where do you begin comes to mind with the loss of a child. It becomes more difficult if it unexpectedly was your proud oldest son. It gets mixed up with other thoughts but begins with Ryan's arrival with Lamaze natural child birth. Ryan in Gaelic means Little King. And like a King Ryan made a grand arrival. Like trumpets the nurses began screaming to hurry up and deliver that baby as the oil terminal nearby blew up! The moment Ryan was born I stared in awe at big orange fireballs of flame from the oil terminal silhouetting across the hospital windows, like a welcome for Ryan the "King" arrival to Earth.

Thoughts of changing Ryan's diapers, was a big memory as the 10 lb. kid was always on diaper overload; and of course sending Ryan off to 1st Grade (for the 2nd time) with Rocky by our side at the bus stop. Ryan the student athlete suddenly had Karate trophies start to pile up in his room along with football, basketball, and baseball awards. Then after begging for a brother and getting 3 gorgeous sisters Ryan finally got his little brother. Eight years later, and he had to share the same room! Suddenly pages of time on the calendar just flew by in a flurry of child rearing and it seemed like we were sending Ryan off to Navy boot camp.

Driving Ryan to his many games was rewarded with watching him win his games! Grandpa Sullivan always went to Ryan's football games, and ran onto the field with a hoodsie ice cream after every game. Ryan & Rocky loved Grandpa Sullivan because he always brought a treat!

While pasting together "Rocky the Awesome Dog" I remembered I should mention the story of Ryan trying to enter Rocky in dog training school at Sandwich, MA Dog Park.

It was an amazing gift to see the look of awe on Ryan's face when the dog trainer handed Rocky's leash to Ryan and told Ryan that "Rocky didn't need to go to dog school!" "Ryan was told Rocky was born very smart and a natural well trained dog." Rocky was born off lease Shutzen trained. It was inbred for Rocky to walk beside Ryan's leg without a leash on because many years of Rocky's family were trained work dogs. Ryan use to laugh and shout out funny things when he played with Rocky. Ryan would joke, "Rocky" was born "smart" like he came right out of a UFO. It was an adorable sight to watch young Ryan shout out praise to Rocky when he would be a good doggie and do what Ryan asked.

For those of you who were little and don't remember much because you were just a kid, I'm writing to share a tidbit so that you know in little ways that your Dad Ryan Sullivan was an Awesome Possum!

Ryan played an important role in the story of "Rocky the Awesome Dog!" Ryan as a young innocent boy gave the love that nurtured the greatness in the little pup "Rocky." For those that knew Ryan they know he loved the outdoors. And all that started in the wooded forest of Cedarville where Ryan taught his dog Rocky to grow up to be truly an awesome dog!"

"Little Corners of the Earth set aside to bring Joy to little Boys!"

Many years ago before Ryan went to 1st grade he walked the Buffalo River in Arkansas with his Daddy finding Indian arrowheads in the River, and looking for a good place to fish.

Ryan found in the Buffalo River Park this message posted on a sign about "little corners of the Earth set aside to bring

Joy to little boys." This story was read to Ryan as he overlooked the Buffalo River where Ryan caught a fish that day!

"There are little corners of this earth put aside by nature to be discovered by and to bring joy to little boys.

The lands over which you look here, across this beautiful river, are such a corner, and the quiet pools to be found there, the tiny box canyon with its waterfall and the springs above, are set aside forever for all little boys!

In memory of another little boy who did discover freedom and joy here."

-Warren Mallory Johnston, Arkansas

*Ryan Patrick Sullivan pictured at Buffalo River Park, Arkansas. The picture was taken by his father Edward, who said, "It was like Ryan personified the Memorial "Joy to little boys" "It was the appearance of Ryan's angelic smile & handsome youth amidst the natural beauty of the Buffalo River where Ryan found great "joy" in catching arrowheads & fish.

US Air Force Veteran Jade Sullivan
US Naval Veteran Ryan Sullivan
At USS Constitution Wharf for WWII Memorial Event
Veterans Day November 11, 2000 Old North Church
Reception Joe Tecce's Restaurant North End Boston
Honored Guest WWII US Naval Armed Guard Ed
Sullivan Sr.,
WWII Memorial Event Chairman Capt. Ed Sullivan Jr.,

A True Celebration of Life
Ryan Sullivan
Ryan in Gaelic: "Little King"
Sullivan in Gaelic: "One eyed Warrior"
December 3, 1979

Grandpa Edward & Grandma Heather Sullivan
San Pedro, California

Ryan Sullivan Baptized – January 1980

Mary Star of the Sea Catholic Church
877 West 7th Street
San Pedro, CA 90731

(L to R) front row: Godmother Rosemary
Holding beside Mother Heather
Marilyn Murray, Sheila Murray Kirby
(L to R) back row: Roberta Browne
Mr. Brown, & Godfather Dave Murray

Ryan receives Sacrament of Confirmation

St. Bonaventure's Catholic Church
799 State Road
Manomet Village
Plymouth, Massachusetts 02360

Ryan confirms middle name "Patrick"
Ryan Patrick Sullivan becomes soldier in God's Army"

A GIFT OF

Healing Masses

Ryan P. Sullivan

is hereby enrolled in

THE TRINITY MISSIONS
MASS SOCIETY

*and will be included in the daily prayers
of the Trinity Missionaries,
Friday Masses, and 12 special Novenas
of Masses including the
Feast of Our Lady of Lourdes*

Fr. Stephen, S.T.

Father Stephen, S.T.
Enrolled by:

Anne M. Sullivan

Jesus, I Trust in You

39

52

Heavenly Father,
bless this family as we journey closer to you
each day. May you always remind us of the
strength we have when we stand together,
united in love and faith.

Help us to open our hearts to one another, to
listen when one of us is crying out, to extend a
hand when one of us is hurting, to rejoice
when one of us has cause for celebration.

Dear Lord,
we are joined forever by our family ties.
We pray that we will never take that for
granted and that we will always find comfort,
acceptance and love at the heart of this family.

Amen.

Enrolled by:

Anne M. Sullivan

✝

With the sympathy of

Rosemary Angelique
(Aunt Rowie)

The

Holy Sacrifice of the Mass

will be offered

for the repose of

the soul of

Ryan Sullivan

Date 12-12-17   Time 8:15 AM

Rev. *Donal Keohane*

St. Martin of Tours Church
11967 Sunset Blvd.
Los Angeles, CA 90049

54

†

With the sympathy of

Elizabeth Reis

The

Holy Sacrifice of the Mass

will be offered

for the repose of

the soul of

Ryan Sullivan

Rev. _____
at

St Patrick Catholic Church, Cranston, RI
on
Saturday, December 23, 2017
5:00 PM

55

Mass Card for Ryan Sullivan

From Aunt MaryAnne Sullivan

Revere, Massachusetts

Chapel to St. Jude & St. Anthony

I am Free

PRAY FOR US

St. Jude and
St. Anthony

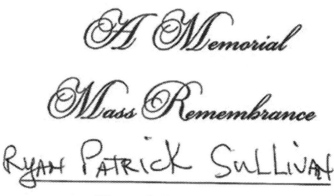

A Memorial
Mass Remembrance

Ryan Patrick Sullivan

will benefit from a perpetual
remembrance in the prayers of the
Salvatorian Fathers and Brothers,
including a special holy Mass
celebrated each day in Rome
at the Motherhouse of the
Society of the Divine Savior.

Given by Jacqueline + Michael Sullivan

Fr. Gregory, S.D.S.

Spiritual Director

Capuchin Mission Association

In Loving Memory

Ryan Sullivan

has been enrolled in the Association
and will share forever in the
Daily Masses, Prayers and Meritorious
Works of the Capuchin Franciscan Friars
throughout the world.

Requested by:

Joan A. Garrett RYAN

Jan 25, 2018

*A*t this sad time

and in the days to come,

hoping you feel

the care of others

holding and sustaining you...

surrounding you always.

Thinking of you...
The Russells
Jon, Cindy, Kim & Barry,
David, Katey & Ellie

With the sympathy of

Eileen + Lenny
Lavallee
With Love,
Eileen (Sullivan) Lavallee
Lenny Lavallee

The

Holy Sacrifice of the Mass

will be offered

for the repose of

the soul of

Michelle + Ryan Sullivan

Rev. Julian P. Harris

St. Thomas More Catholic Church
10935 South Military Trail
Boynton Beach, FL 33436

In Loving Memory

Perpetual Enrollment
in the
Spiritual Treasury
of the
Companions of St. Anthony
has been granted to

Ryan Sullivan

who will share in Special Masses,
as well as the prayers, sacrifices
and good works of the
Franciscan Friars Conventual

at the request of

Companions of St. Anthony Staff

on this _5th_ day of _December 2017_

Father Richard-Jacob Forcier, OFM Conv.
Spiritual Guardian

61

Miscellaneous pictures of Ryan Sullivan

"Going Down Memory Lane"

Plymouth, the Land of Plenty!
Ryan Sullivan seen with two of his three CJ Jeeps that he had between September and November of his Senior year at Plymouth South High School. Ryan loved his Jeeps!

Ryan's 1st fish in the Buffalo River!

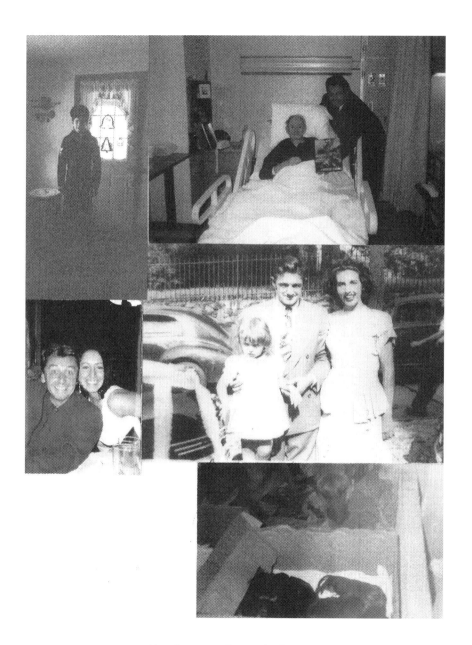

Shadow and Rocky's Pup

Student's Name _RYAN SULLIVAN_
Address _57 ROXY CAHOON RD.,_
Town _PLYMOUTH_ Tel. _888-8579_
Name of your SCHOOL_INDIAN BROOK_
Name of your TEACHER_MRS. FLYNN_
What grade are you in? _2ND_
My SCHOOL PICTURE ORDER IS_PACK "B"_. My payment

NATURAL COLOR SCHOOL MEMORY PICTUI

69

Ryan with Mom's Shadow

Ryan Sullivan, Captain
Plymouth South Panthers
Football Team

Falmouth Green Pond - Ryan tying
dingy Ave' Maria to sailboat Natasha!
Off to Martha's Vineyard – Steer 180 degrees south!

About the Author - Rocky the Awesome Dog!

Capt. Ed Sullivan, was blessed to have the wonderful experience of bringing together his son Ryan and his dog Rocky to enjoy their youthful days together in the forest of America's hometown Plymouth, Massachusetts.

Capt. Ed Sullivan is the author of "Daddy's Not Comin' Home," and to soon be released from Author House "Mommy Went to Work." Historical fiction stories of the merchant marine sailors who incurred the highest casualty rate in WWII, and the women who built the largest fleet of ships in the history of the world helping to preserve our American way of life.

Ryan Sullivan "Rocky's" master had distinguished service in the US Navy carrying on a tradition of over a century of service by the Sullivan family.

The author rededicated the story of "Rocky the Awesome Dog," for his grandchildren Declan and Jack to include his son Ryan and the gift this June of his newly born daughter "Ryan" named after her father.

With the world today filled with indifference and misunderstandings, the author shares this story with the reader to instill the importance of joyful memories in our youth as we reflect on our journey in life.

Printed in the United States
By Bookmasters